Maxims and Counsels of
St. Francis De Sales
For Every Day of the Year

Maxims and Counsels of St. Francis De Sales

For Every Day of the Year

by Saint Francis De Sales

Translated by Ella Mcmahon

INTRODUCTION

Pious Soul:

The Spiritual Father who presents himself to you under this title is the gentle Bishop of Geneva, who, in the opinion of St. Jane Chantal and St. Vincent de Paul, was the most perfect imitation of our Saviour living among men.

Love for souls is his great passion. He is not astonished at either falls or discouragement, which he cures by remedies as gentle as they are efficacious. Whatever your disposition you will find sometimes a word of consolation, sometimes a counsel of perfection, or a means of accomplishing a difficult step in the ways of God, and of elevating yourself to Him.

This collection is like the inner life of the Saint unconsciously written by himself. He first practised, and then taught. One is gentle from motives of virtue, only when he possesses moral strength; now we find in these lines the secret of that strength which made St. Francis de Sales the gentlest of men. He admirably inculcates the method of sanctity which he perfectly possessed—a sanctity which seems so easy to realise that we feel a desire to reproduce it. It is the flower which the Spiritual Father causes to bloom in your soul. It will soon bear fruit if you are faithful.

These counsels have been carefully gleaned from the complete collection of the holy Doctor.

1.

Keep yourself faithfully in the presence of God; avoid hurry and anxiety, for there are no greater obstacles to our progress in perfection.

2.

Cast your heart gently, not violently, into the wounds of our Saviour; have an unlimited confidence in his mercy and goodness.

3.

To make good progress we must devote ourselves to getting over that portion of the path which lies close before us, and not amuse ourselves with the desire to attain the last step before we have accomplished the first.

4.

We must make our imperfections die with us from day to day. Dear imperfections, which cause us to recognise our misery, which exercise us in contempt of self, and the practice of virtue, and notwithstanding which God accepts the preparation of our hearts which is perfect.

5.

I recommend simplicity to you; look before you, and not at the dangers which you behold in the distance. Keep your will firmly bent upon serving

God with your whole heart. While you are thus occupied in forecasting the future you expose yourself to some false step.

6.

Have no care for the morrow; think only of doing well to-day, and when to-morrow shall have become to-day then we shall think about it.

7.

We must make a provision of manna for each day only; and let us not be afraid that God will fail to send down more upon us to-morrow and the day after to-morrow, and every day of our pilgrimage.

8.

Since the Heart of our Lord has no more loving law than meekness, humility, and charity we must firmly maintain these dear virtues in us.

9.

True sanctity lies in love of God, and not in foolish imaginings, raptures, &c. Let us devote ourselves to the practice of true meekness and submission, to renouncement of self, to docility of heart, to love of abjection, to consideration for the wishes of others: this is true sanctity and the most amiable ecstasy of the children of God.

10.

May you belong to God for ever in this mortal life, serving Him faithfully through its trials, bearing the cross after Him, and may you be his for ever in life eternal with the whole celestial court!

11.

The great good of our souls is to live for God, and the greatest good to live for God alone.

12.

He who lives but for God is never sad, save at having offended God.

13.

He who lives but for God seeks only God, and since God is with him in adversity as well as in prosperity, he dwells in peace in the midst of tribulation.

14.

He who lives but for God frequently thinks of Him during all the occupations of life.

15.

Then let us belong wholly to Him, and live but for Him, desiring only to please Him, and for his creatures in Him, through Him, and for Him.

16.

Make your little efforts sweetly, peacefully, and amiably to please this Sovereign Goodness, and do not be astonished at difficulties.

17.

We must be constant in aspiring to the perfection of holy love, in order that love may be perfect; for the love which seeks anything less than perfection cannot fail to be imperfect.

18.

Never permit your soul to be sad and live in bitterness of spirit or scrupulous fear, since He who loved it and died to give it life is so good, so sweet, so amiable.

19.

To live contentedly in our exile, we must keep before our eyes the hope of our arrival in the country where we shall live for ever.

20.

God, who calls us to Him, sees how we are approaching, and will never permit anything to happen but what is for our greater good.

21.

God knows what we are, and will hold out his paternal hand to us in a difficult step, in order that nothing may arrest us.

22.

Never look forward to the accidents of life with apprehension; anticipate them with a perfect hope that God, whose child you are, will deliver you from them, according as they come.

23.

God has preserved you so far; only keep yourself faithful to the law of his providence and He will assist you at all times, and where you cannot walk He will carry you.

24.

Do not think of what may happen to-morrow, for the same eternal Father who cares for you to-day will care for you to-morrow and always; either He will not send you trouble, or, if He does, He will give you invincible courage to bear it.

25.

The child can never perish who remains in the arms of a Father who is almighty.

26.

If God does not always give us what we ask, it is to keep us near Him and give us an opportunity to urge and constrain Him by a loving violence.

27.

Behold this great Artisan of mercy. He converts our miseries into graces and the poison of our iniquities into salutary remedies for our souls. Tell me, I pray, what will He not do with the afflictions, the labours, the persecutions which assail us?

28.

An over-sensitive mind can neither receive nor endure anything without telling of it, and it is always a little astonished at the lowly places which humility and simplicity choose.

29.

I see you with your vigorous heart which loves and wills powerfully. I like it, for what are those half-dead hearts good for? We must make a particular exercise once every week of willing to love the will of God more tenderly, more affectionately than anything in the world, and that, too, not only in bearable but in the most unbearable events.

30.

Even at a time when you had not so much confidence in God, did you perish in affliction? Then why have you not courage to meet all other trials?

31.

Plant in your heart Jesus Christ Crucified, and all the crosses of this world will seem to you like roses.

32.

We must not only be willing that God should strike us, but we must accept that He shall strike us where He wills.

33.

Lord Jesus, without reserve, without an if, without a but, without exception, without limitation, may thy holy will be done in all things, at all times.

34.

Daily strengthen yourself more and more in the resolution, which you formed with so much affection: of serving God according to his good pleasure.

35.

Never think you have attained the purity of heart which you owe to God until your will is freely and joyfully resigned to his holy will in all things, even in the most repugnant.

36.

Regard not the appearance of the things you are to do, but Him who commands them, and who, when He pleases, can accomplish his glory and our perfection through the most imperfect and trifling things.

37.

A true servant of God has no care for the morrow; he performs faithfully what is required of him to-day, and to-morrow he will do what is required of him without a word.

38.

So, no matter how God treats you, it is all the same to you, you tell me.... Ah! how suddenly self-love insinuates itself into our affections, however devout they may appear.

39.

Here is the great lesson: We must discover God's will, and, recognising it, we must endeavour to do it joyfully, or at least courageously.

40.

The meek Saviour would have us meek, so that, though surrounded by the world and the flesh, we may live by the Spirit; that, amidst the vanities of earth, we may live in heaven; that, living among men, we may praise Him with the angels.

41.

The sight alone of our dear Jesus crucified can speedily soften all sorrows, which are but flowers compared with his thorns. And then our great rendezvous is an eternal heaven; and compared with the price of eternity, what are the things which end with time?

42.

Continue to unite yourself more and more with our Lord. Plunge your heart into the charity of his, and say always with your whole soul: "May I die and may Jesus live!" Our death will be a happy one if we have died daily.

43.

The repugnance you feel testifies no want of love; for it seems to me that, if we believed that being flayed God would love us more we would flay ourselves, not without repugnance, but in spite of the repugnance.

44.

Cultivate not only a solid love, but a tender, gentle, meek love for those about you; I have learned from experience that infirmities destroy, not our charity, but our meekness towards our neighbour, if we are not strongly on our guard.

45.

Lord Jesus, what true happiness for a soul consecrated to God to be strongly exercised in tribulation before leaving this life!

46.

How can we know frank, ardent love but in the midst of thorns, crosses, weariness, above all, when this weariness is prolonged?

47.

Nothing can give us deeper peace in this world than to frequently contemplate our Lord in all the afflictions He endured from his birth to his death: contempt, calumnies, poverty, abjection, weariness, suffering, nakedness, wrongs, and grief of every kind.

48.

A heart which esteems and grandly loves Jesus crucified, loves his death, his sufferings, his insults, his poverty, his hunger, his thirst; and when Jesus grants this heart a small share in them, it is jubilant with gladness and lovingly embraces them.

49.

Every day, not in prayer, but in your walks, you should recall to mind our Lord amid the thorns of our redemption, and consider what happiness it would be to share them.

50.

Let us faithfully cultivate that resignation and pure love of God which is never wholly practised but amid sufferings; for to love God, when He feeds us with sweetness is nothing more than children do; but to love Him when He feeds us with gall is to offer Him the cup of our loving fidelity.

51.

I recommend you to God, that you may obtain the gift of holy patience; and it is not in my power to propose to Him anything for you, save that He may, according to his holy will, fashion your heart for his dwelling, and reign there eternally; and whether He fashion it with the brush, the hammer, or the chisel, must be according to his good pleasure.

52.

The heart which unites itself to the Heart of God cannot help loving and accepting with sweetness the arrows with which God pierces it.

53.

I desire that your cross and mine should be wholly the cross of Jesus Christ; and as to the imposition of this or that burden, or making any choice, God knows what He is doing and why He does it—it is certainly for our good.

54.

Our sweet Saviour is pleased that we should speak to Him of the trouble He sends us, and that we should complain, provided it be lovingly and humbly, and to Himself, just as little children do when their mother has punished them.

55.

God wishes that, like Job, I should serve Him in the midst of dryness, suffering, and temptation; like St. Paul, that I should serve Him according to his desire. You will see that one day He will do all and even more than you can desire.

56.

I praise God for the constancy with which you bear tribulations. Nevertheless I still see in you a little over-eagerness and restlessness which form an obstacle to the final effect of your patience.

57.

The effect of patience is to possess one's soul, and, in proportion to our patience do we acquire complete and perfect possession of our soul.

58.

We must lose everything rather than courage, confidence, and goodwill.

59.

Would to God that we paid little attention to the condition of the road which alarms us, but kept our eyes steadily fixed upon Him who guides us, and the happy end to which He leads us.

60.

When you have meditated upon the grievous anguish which our Master endured in the Garden, and in union with Him prayed to the Father for consolation, if it does not please Him to send it, think no more of it, but brace your courage to work out your salvation on the cross, as if you were never to descend therefrom, and as if you were never to see the atmosphere of your life clear and serene.

61.

For the honour of God yield completely to his will, and do not think that you can serve Him better another way, for we serve Him well only when we serve Him as He wills.

62.

We are always wishing for this or that, and though we have our sweet Jesus in our breasts, we are not content. Yet it is all we can desire. One thing alone is necessary, and that is, to be near Him.

63.

Train yourself to serve our Lord with a strong and fervent gentleness: it is the true way of serving Him.

64.

Frequently kiss in your heart the crosses which our Lord Himself has placed in your arms. Heed not whether they are of perfumed or precious wood: they are more truly crosses when they are of coarse, heavy, ordinary wood.

65.

This sweet love of our hearts casts us down only to raise us up. He lurks and hides, peeping through the lattice, to see the expression of our countenance.

66.

Keep Jesus closely in your arms, for it is thus the Spouse holds Him as a bouquet of myrrh, that is of bitterness: but He is not bitter; He only allows us to be bitter to ourselves.

67.

Being a good servant of God is not always having consolation and sweetness, nor being always free from aversion and repugnance to good.

68.

To be a good servant of God is to be charitable to our neighbour, maintaining in the superior will an invincible resolution to do God's will: to possess great humility and simplicity in confiding one's self to God; to rise as frequently as one falls; to inure one's self to humiliations, and to tranquilly bear with others and their defects.

69.

Frequently behold our Lord who looks down upon you, poor little creature that you are, and sees you in the midst of your labours and distractions.

70.

Frequently raise your heart to God, ask his help, and let the foundation of your consolation be the happiness of belonging to Him.

71.

Let us raise up our hearts, and behold that of God all goodness, all love, all love for us! Let us adore and bless his will in all things, let Him prune, let Him cut where He will, for we are eternally his.

72.

Let us place ourselves before our Crucified Sun, as the weary bee basks in the rays of the sun, and then let us say to Him: "O beautiful Sun of hearts, Thou dost vivify all by the rays of thy goodness; behold us exhausted before thee, whence we will not move, Lord Jesus, until Thy fire hath revived us!"

73.

Let us not forget the maxim of the saints, which warns us that every day we must feel that we begin our perfection; and if we bear this well in mind we will not be astonished at the miseries we find in ourselves. The work is never done, it must be always recommenced; and recommenced with a good heart.

74.

What we are about to commence will be better than what we have done, and when we shall have accomplished that, we will recommence something else which shall be still better, and then something else, until we leave this world to begin another life, which will have no end, for nothing, nothing better can come to us.

75.

See, then, whether one should weep when he finds trouble in his soul, and whether he ought not courageously to push on ever further, since he must never pause, and whether he ought not to have the resolution to prune, since we must use the knife, even to the division of soul and mind.

76.

Why do you weep, O woman? No, you must no longer be a woman, you must have the heart of a man. But courage! take heart! we have our sweet Jesus with us.

77.

The love of God does not consist in consolations, otherwise our Lord would not have loved his Father when He was sorrowful unto death, and when He cried, "My God, my God, why hast Thou forsaken me?" This was the greatest act of love which it is possible to imagine.

78.

Our imperfections should not please us, but they should not take away our courage. God does not like our imperfections and venial sins, but He loves us in spite of them.

79.

Live joyfully; our Lord looks down upon you, and looks upon you with love, and with a tenderness proportioned to your foolishness.

80.

Turn your eyes from yourself, and direct them towards God with an humble courage to speak to Him of his ineffable goodness in loving our poor human nature, in spite of its infirmities.

81.

Our enemy is a great bawler; be in no way troubled about him, for he cannot hurt you; despise him, and pay no attention to him. He made as much noise and thundered as loudly about the saints; but behold! they are lodged in the place which the miserable creature lost.

82.

Fear not; you are walking upon the sea, amid the winds and the waves, but it is with Jesus. If fear seizes you, cry loudly, "Lord, save me!" He will stretch forth his hand to you; clasp it firmly and go joyfully on.

83.

Despise, I pray you, all those thoughts of vainglory. For they are really but flies which cannot harm but only annoy you. It is an incompatible thing to be in this world and not to feel the movements of the passions.

84.

Let yourself be governed by God; do not think so much of yourself.

85.

I expressly forbid you to be over-eager, as this is the mother imperfection of all imperfections.

86.

Simplify your judgment. "If your eye is simple, your whole body will be light." Do not make so many reflections and replies, but go on with simplicity and confidence.

87.

For you there are but God and yourself in the world, and you should not concern yourself for all the rest, save as God commands you.

88.

Give your soul a thousand times to God, and sometimes say not a word to Him, but simply contemplate his gentleness. This is one of the great sources of spiritual gain, for as the mind converses so frequently and so easily with its God it will be perfumed with all his perfections.

89.

The Christian soul is the spouse not yet of Jesus glorified, but of Jesus crucified; that is why the rings, ornaments, and tokens with which He adorns her are crosses, and thorns, and the nuptial banquet is gall, hyssop, and vinegar.

90.

Do not look here and there so much. Turn your eyes upon God or yourself; you will never see God without goodness, or yourself free from misery; and you will find his goodness kind to your misery, and your misery the object of his mercy.

91.

Rarely examine closely what others do; look upon them simply, kindly, and amiably. Do like the bees, gather honey from all the flowers.

92.

My commandment is, that you do like little children; while they feel their mother holding them by the sleeve, they go on boldly and run about everywhere, nothing daunted by the falls that are caused by the weakness of their legs. Thus, while God holds you by your good-will to serve Him, go on boldly, undaunted by your little stumblings, provided you cast yourself into his arms and give Him the kiss of charity.

93.

Go joyously and with a light heart as far as you can, and if you cannot always go joyously, go always courageously and confidently.

94.

We must have patience, and little by little, correct and overcome our bad habits, for life on the whole is a continual warfare.

95.

Rest is reserved for heaven; on earth we must always struggle between hope and fear, on condition that hope be ever the stronger when we consider the almighty power of Him who helps us.

96.

Frequently during the day cast your heart, your mind, and your care upon God with great confidence, saying, "I am thine, save me."

97.

Be kind to your neighbour in spite of rebellious murmurings and outbursts of anger.

98.

Do not be astonished to find yourself overwhelmed with evil inclinations. God permits them in order to make you humble.

99.

Self-love may be mortified in us, but it never dies; from time to time it sends forth shoots which prove that, though cut down to the root, it is never completely destroyed.

100.

Self-love never leaves us. It sleeps sometimes like a fox, then suddenly springs upon the chickens. We must therefore be constantly watchful of it, and patiently defend ourselves against it.

101.

Let us keep firm hold of the merciful hand of our good God, for He wishes to draw us after Him.

102.

Live wholly according to the Spirit, live quietly in peace, have perfect confidence that God will help you.

103.

Be careful to purify your heart more and more each day. Now, this purity consists in weighing everything in the scales of the sanctuary, which are only the will of God.

104.

Let us be what we are, and be that well, in order that we may honour the Master Workman who has made us. Though we were the most excellent creatures under heaven, what would it avail us if we were not pleasing to the will of God?

105.

We must always and in all things live peaceably.

106.

I approve of your making an act of humility every day, humbling yourself to an inferior, performing some menial office in the house.

107.

It is not possible that you should so soon be mistress of your soul, or that you should control it so absolutely at first.

108.

Dispose your soul to tranquillity in the morning, and be careful during the day to recall it frequently to that state, and to keep your soul within your control.

109.

Do not be terrified if you are guilty of some little impatience; do not let it trouble you, but when you recognise it quietly humble yourself before God.

110.

Try to preserve a sweet tranquillity of mind; say to your soul: "Courage! we have made a false step, but let us keep steadily on and keep watch over ourselves."

111.

Make no account of the judgments of men.

112.

Be silent concerning all things, and you will have interior peace, because for you and me the only secret of acquiring this peace is to endure to the utmost the judgments of men.

113.

Consider for whom you labour, and those who strive to trouble you shall labour in vain.

114.

Among beggars, those whose sores are the most terrible consider themselves the most fortunate, for they excite more compassion and receive more abundant alms. We are only beggars, and the most miserable among us are the most fortunate, for these God looks upon with greater compassion.

115.

Be glad that men make no account of you.

116.

Consider how all the vexations of the past have vanished; those of the future shall vanish in the same way.

117.

The great point of humility is to see, to honour, to serve, and converse fittingly with those whom we dislike, keeping ourselves humble, gentle, and submissive to them, for remember that the humiliations which are the least visible are the keenest.

118.

Let our Lord turn us to the left or to the right, and send us in a hundred directions. He never abandons us but to get closer possession of us; He never leaves us but to guard us better; He never struggles with us but to enter our souls and bless us.

119.

Courage! Let us keep on in the low valleys of the small and humble virtues. I love these three little virtues: gentleness of heart, firmness of mind, and simplicity of life.

120.

I recommend to you more than anything else the exercise of holy gentleness and sweetness in all the events of this life.

121.

Accustom yourself in all that you do to act and speak gently and quietly, and you will see that in three or four years you will completely control that abrupt impulsiveness.

122.

He who can preserve peace in the midst of the confusion and complexity of business, and sweetness in the midst of suffering, is almost perfect.

123.

I recommend to you great evenness of temper, sweetness and gentleness of heart; for these virtues, like the oil of a lamp, maintain the flame of good example; for there is nothing more edifying to our neighbour than charitable kindliness.

124.

When shall we be wholly imbued with sweetness and gentleness towards our neighbour? You needed only that; your zeal was good, but it had this fault; it was a little bitter, over-urgent, and captious.

125.

Raise your eyes to heaven, and among the mortals now immortal there you will not find one who attained eternal happiness but through continual afflictions and trouble.

126.

Let us humble ourselves profoundly, and acknowledge that if God be not our shield and armour, we shall be pierced through and through with every kind of sin.

127.

I desire that you should be extremely lowly and humble in your own eyes, condescending and gentle as a dove.

128.

Do not be quick to speak; say much by a modest and judicious silence.

129.

Behold God in all things without exception, acquiescing in all his commands with great simplicity.

130.

Say frequently, in the midst of your contradictions and sufferings: This is the path to heaven; I behold the gate, and I am sure that the storms will not prevent my reaching it.

131.

Take no trouble on account of what the world thinks of you; despise its good opinion and its contempt, and let it say what it will of good or evil.

132.

Do not think that our Lord is further from you in the midst of turmoil.... It is not tranquillity which brings Him to our hearts, but the fidelity of our love.

133.

From day to day withdraw your heart from all kinds of amusement and vanity, ... from all that turns you from a blessed eternity.

134.

I desire to love God or die; death or love, for life without love is worse than death.

135.

O God! it is towards Thee that I am sailing.... We reach the port through all storms, provided we have an upright heart, a good intention, firm courage, our eyes fixed upon God, and all our confidence in Him.

136.

Do not be vexed at the annoyances which come from the complexity of business; believe me, true virtue is not nourished in exterior repose any more than good fish in stagnant water.

137.

Keep your hearts well under control, beware of over-anxiety. Place your confidence in the providence of our Lord. Be fully convinced that heaven and earth shall pass away rather than that our Lord shall fail to protect you while you are his obedient daughter, or, at least, desirous to obey Him.

138.

Live wholly in our Lord, let Him be the atmosphere in which your heart breathes at ease.

139.

Give particular attention to the practice of gentleness, study every pulsation of your heart, and if it be not gentle, make it so before all things.

140.

I desire that upon all occasions during the day you should interiorly recollect yourself in God, addressing Him a few words of fidelity and love.

141.

Believe me, God loves souls shaken by storms, provided they receive all from his hands and valiantly strive to remain faithful in the midst of combats.

142.

One of the best penances and satisfactions which a heart guilty of some fault can offer is to endure a continual cross and abnegation of its self-love.

143.

It gives me an incomparable pleasure to think of the great honour it is for a soul to speak heart to heart with its God—that great, sovereign infinite Being—yes, for what the heart says to God is known only to God Himself. Is not this a marvellous secret!

144.

When we pray it is well to think that there is no one in the world but God.

145.

The great secret in prayer is simply to follow the attractions of the heart. We must go on in good faith and with pure intention to reach God, to love Him, and unite ourselves to Him. True love has little method.

146.

You should be so in love with God that even though you can do nothing in his presence, you should nevertheless be glad to be near Him, were it only to see Him and look at Him from time to time.

147.

When your heart is distracted in prayer, bring it gently back to the point from which it has wandered, and lay it tenderly at the feet of its Master. If you do but this your hour will be well employed.

148.

If we can speak to our Lord in prayer let us speak to Him, praise Him, listen to Him. If we cannot speak because we are spiritually hoarse, let us stay nevertheless and make Him a reverence.

149.

What a happiness it is to be with God, no one knowing what passes between God and the heart but God Himself and the adoring heart.

150.

I should like to have a good hammer with which to blunt the sharpness of your mind, which is too subtle in its ideas of your advancement. I have often told you that in devotion we must go on in good faith, acting frankly and promptly. If you do well, praise God; if ill, humble yourself.

151.

Humble yourself profoundly, and urge on your soul with the love of Christ crucified, that you may be able to spiritually digest this heavenly food.

152.

He who communicates according to the spirit of the Spouse annihilates himself before God, saying to our Lord: Destroy me, annihilate me, and convert me into Thee; then it is no longer we who live, but Jesus Christ, who liveth in us.

153.

When the mother pearl has received the drops of the fresh morning dew it draws within itself and closes its shell to preserve them fresh; in like manner, when you have received the Blessed Sacrament, withdraw into yourself and collect all the faculties of your soul to adore this sovereign King, and relish by a lively faith the spiritual refreshment which this Divine Germ produces in your breast.

154.

Take your rest as much as possible near the heavenly Infant. See how He receives the breath of that great ox and that ass, which neither feel his presence nor show it by any movement. Will He not then receive the inspirations of our poor hearts?

155.

How happy we should be had we only Jesus in our understanding, only Jesus in our imagination! Jesus would be in us everywhere, and we everywhere in Jesus.

156.

We should manage our years, our months, our weeks, our days, our hours, our moments so well that, being employed for the love of God, they all may be profitable to us for eternal life.

157.

Shall we not, in future, cease to be the old selves, which shall all, without exception, be for ever sacrificed unreservedly and unconditionally to God and his love?

158.

When you encounter things which give you trouble, remember that the saints cheerfully did greater and more troublesome tasks, and encourage yourself by their example.

159.

A person who is free from the fever of her own will is satisfied with everything, provided God be served. She is indifferent to the nature of the service which God chooses to give her.

160.

Frequently say to our Lord: What wilt Thou that I do? Is it Thy will that I should serve Thee in the most lowly duties of the house? Provided I serve Thee, I care not what the service may be.

161.

Love this good God in your retreats, in Holy Communion, and when He consoles you; love Him particularly in the midst of trouble and confusion, in aridity, contradictions, and tribulations; for it was thus He loved you in the midst of the scourging, the nails, the thorns, the darkness of Calvary.

162.

The monastery is a hospital of spiritual sick who desire to be cured, and to this end submit themselves to the knife, to the lancet, to be burned, to be bled, and to all kinds of bitter remedies. O my very dear daughter, firmly resolve that you will submit to all this, and pay no attention to what self-love may urge to the contrary, but sweetly, amiably, and lovingly take the blessed resolution: to die or to be cured.

163.

Must you be disquieted and troubled because of difficulties? Oh, by no means. It is the devil who is ferreting and spying about your mind, to see if he cannot find some door open to him.

164.

You are right not to care what is said of you; you who belong to God should not think of reputation. Let God dispose of our life, our reputation, and our honour as He pleases, since they are all his. If our humiliations be his glory, are we not glorified?

165.

When you meet with contradictions or afflictions through anyone, beware of yielding to complaints, but compel your heart to suffer tranquilly; if some sudden outburst of impatience escape you, bring your heart back to sweetness and peace.

166.

See, my daughter, we are too fastidious in calling poor a state in which we endure neither hunger, nor cold, nor ignominy, but merely some inconvenience in our plans.

167.

Gradually temper the vivacity of your mind to patience, sweetness, humility, and affability, in the midst of the silliness and imperfections of your sisters.

168.

Nothing gives us profound tranquillity in this world but to frequently look upon our Lord in all his sufferings. In comparison with all that He endured, we shall see that we are wrong to call the little accidents which we encounter afflictions, and that we do not need patience for things so trifling, since a little modesty would suffice to make us bear well all that happens to us.

169.

We must never answer temptations, nor appear to hear the enemy. If he is noisy, patience! we must prostrate ourselves before God and remain at his feet. He will understand that we want his assistance, though we may not be able to speak.

170.

Believe me, my dear daughter, sweets engender worms in little children; that is why our Lord mixes bitter with the sweet for us. We must have a great courage, which on all occasions will resolutely cry, God be praised! caring little for sweet or bitter, light or darkness. Let us keep on in this essential love.

171.

God desires that you serve Him without relish or feeling, in the midst of aversions and afflictions of mind. This service will not give you satisfaction, but it will content Him; it will not be to your taste but it will be to his.

172.

God is so good that He will visit your soul interiorly, and strengthen and establish it in solid humility, simplicity, and mortification.

173.

Let us always keep on; however slow our progress we are getting over a great deal of the road. God wishes that our misery should be the throne of his mercy.

174.

Keep your heart brave and ready for any service that shall be imposed upon it; according as you undertake many things for God, He will second you and work with you.

175.

Have the heart of a child; a will of wax, and a mind free from the slavery of all affection.

176.

Oh, what a great blessing it is, my daughter, to be pliable and easily turned to any service. Our Lord has taught us this submission by his example, as much as by his words.

177.

He who is very attentive to please the heavenly lover has no leisure for introspection; his mind continually tends whither love leads him.

178.

This exercise of the continual abandonment of one's self to the hands of God includes in the most excellent manner all other exercises in their greatest simplicity, purity, and perfection, and while God leaves us the desire for it we should not change it.

179.

Simplicity is an act of charity pure and simple, which considers only God. It looks straight at God, and can suffer no mixture of self-interest nor intermingling of creatures; God alone is its object.

180.

We should bear tenderly with those whom our Lord bears with, we must bow our heads, and bear ourselves contrary to our habits and inclinations.

181.

Complain as little as possible of injuries, for it rarely happens that one complains without sin, since our self-love exaggerates in our eyes and hearts the wrongs we have received.

182.

Hold the cross of our Lord upon your breast, and as long as you firmly clasp it in your arms, the enemy will be at your feet.

183.

Great evenness of temper, continual gentleness and suavity of heart, are more rare than perfect chastity, yet very desirable.

184.

As regards our perfection, which consists in the union of our soul with the Divine Goodness, it is only a question of knowing little and doing much.

185.

We must make up our minds to two things: one is, that we shall find bad weeds growing in our garden, and the other, that we will have the courage to uproot them, for our self-love will live as long as we do, and from it arises all this noxious growth.

186.

We must endeavour to double, not our desires and our exercises, but the perfection with which we fulfil them, seeking by this means to gain more by one action than we would by a hundred others done according to our inclination and affection.

187.

One act performed in dryness of spirit is worth more than several done in great sensible fervour.

188.

I say, then, that we must die in order that God may live in us, for it is impossible to acquire union with God by any other means than mortification. These words, "We must die," are hard, but they are followed by a great sweetness, and this sweetness is union with God.

189.

Your miseries and infirmities should not astonish you; God has seen many others, and his mercy does not reject the miserable, but is exercised in doing them good.

190.

We must do everything through a motive of love, and nothing through compulsion. Our love for obedience must be greater than our fear of disobedience.

191.

I leave you liberty of spirit, not that which excludes obedience, but that which excludes constraint, scruple, or over-eagerness.

192.

Here are the marks of true liberty: 1st. The heart which possesses this liberty is not attached to consolations, but receives afflictions with all the sweetness that the flesh admits of. I do not say that it does not love and desire consolations, but that the heart is not bound to them.

193.

2nd. Such a heart is in no way attached to spiritual exercises, so that if sickness or any other accident interferes with them it feels no regret. I also do not say that it does not love them, but that it is not attached to them.

194.

3rd. Such a heart rarely loses its joy, for no privation saddens one whose heart is not bound to anything. I do not say that it never loses its joy, but that it is only for a short time.

195.

A soul which possesses true liberty will leave his prayer, and with an amiable countenance and gracious manner greet the importunate person who disturbs him. For it is the same to him whether he serve God in meditation or by bearing with his neighbour; they are both the will of God.

196.

Liberty of spirit has two vices: a spirit of inconstancy and a spirit of constraint. For example: I resolve to make a meditation every morning. If I have a spirit of inconstancy I will defer it till evening at the slightest excuse —for the barking of a dog which has disturbed my sleep, for a letter to be written, though it is not at all urgent. On the contrary, if I have a spirit of constraint I will not omit my meditation, even though a sick person is very much in need of my services.

197.

Everything tends to the good of those who love God. And, in truth, since God can draw good from evil, for whom will He do it, if not for those who have given themselves without reserve to Him? Yes, everything tends to their profit, even sin. David would never have been so humble if he had not sinned; nor would Magdalene's love for her Saviour have been what it was. Tell me, then, what will He not do with our afflictions and labours?

198.

If, then, it ever happen that some grief come upon you, assure your soul that if she love God all things will turn to her good. And though you may not see the means by which this good shall be effected, be all the more convinced of it.

199.

It is a very good sign that the enemy rages and beats at your door: it shows that he has not what he wants. If he had he would cease to cry out, but would quietly enter and stay with you.

200.

Courage! As long as we can say, even coldly, God be praised, there is no reason to fear. And do not tell me that it seems to you that you say it in a spiritless way, with no strength or courage, but as if you had to do violence to yourself to utter it. Oh, this is the blessed violence which taketh heaven!

201.

As long as a temptation is displeasing to you there is nothing to fear, for why does it displease you if not because you do not wish it?

202.

Moreover, these very importunate temptations come from the malice of the devil, but the trouble and suffering they cause us come from the mercy of God. He draws from the malice of his enemy the holy tribulation by which He refines the gold He desires to place in his treasury. Despise the temptations and embrace the tribulations.

203.

We must endure our own want of perfection, if we would attain perfection. I say that we must endure it patiently, but we must not love or caress it. It is by the endurance of this suffering that humility is nourished.

204.

Those who aspire to pure love of God have not so much need of patience with others as with themselves.

205.

We must confess the truth: we are poor creatures, capable of very little that is good; but God, who is infinitely good, is content with our poor labours, and finds acceptable the preparation of our heart.

206.

But what means this preparation of our heart according to the expression of Holy Writ: "God is greater than our heart, and our heart is greater than the world?" When our heart, in the solitude of meditation, prepares the service which it must render God, it effects marvels. All this preparation, nevertheless, is in no way proportioned to the grandeur of God, and ordinarily it exceeds our strength, and becomes too great to be carried out in our exterior actions.

207.

Our minds prepare for God a mortified flesh free from the rebellion of the senses, prayer free from distraction, a loving heart free from all bitterness, a humility free from all taint of vanity. All this is very good, an excellent preparation; but who carries it out? Alas! when we come to the practise of it, we fall short. Must we on this account be disquieted, troubled, or afflicted? No, certainly not. Must we apply ourselves to exciting a multitude of desires to stimulate ourselves to attain this perfection? By no means.

208.

I do not say that we must not tend to perfection; but we must not desire to attain it in a day, that is in a day of this mortal life, for such a desire would only uselessly disquiet us.

209.

It is not possible, I assure you, to be completely rid of self while we are on earth. We must always carry self with us, until God carries us to heaven; and while we carry self, we carry a burden of very little value.

210.

Solomon tells us that a servant who suddenly becomes mistress is a very insolent creature. Were a soul to become all at once perfect mistress of passions which it had long served, I fear it could not but be vain and proud.

211.

If in our heart there be a single thread of affection which is not for God, we should instantly tear it out.

212.

I cannot understand how you, a daughter of God, long since abandoned to the bosom of his mercy and consecrated to his love, can yield to such immoderate sadness. You should console yourself, despising all the mournful and melancholy suggestions with which the devil tries to weary you.

213.

Do not examine yourself so carefully to discover whether you are in perfection or not; for, should we attain the greatest perfection we should neither know nor recognise it, but always consider ourselves imperfect. The end of our examen should never be to discover whether we are imperfect, for that we should never doubt.

214.

Therefore we should never be astonished at imperfection or let it sadden us; for we cannot fail to find ourselves imperfect in this life, and there is no remedy for it save humility, since by this virtue we shall repair our faults and gradually improve.

215.

It is for the exercise of this virtue that our imperfections are left to us, since it is inexcusable not to seek to correct them, and excusable not to succeed perfectly; for it is not with imperfections as it is with sins.

216.

If you wish to do well, regard as a temptation every suggestion concerning change of place; for while your mind is looking beyond where it should be, it will never apply itself to doing well the duty which lies before it.

217.

We must not desire all to begin by perfection. It matters little how one begins, provided he be resolved to go on well, and end well.

218.

I tell you that you will be faithful if you are humble. But will you be humble? Yes, if you wish it. But I do wish it. Then you are humble. But I feel that I am not. So much the better; that helps to make you more so.

219.

You desire that it should always be spring in your soul, but that cannot be. We must endure vicissitudes of weather interiorly as well as exteriorly. It is only in heaven that we shall find the perpetual beauty of spring, the perpetual ripening of summer, the perpetual fruition of autumn. There we shall have no winter; but here winter is required for the exercise of abnega- tion, and a thousand little virtues which are practised in times of sterility.

220.

My God! We shall soon be in eternity, and then we shall see how unim- portant are all the things of this world, and how little it mattered whether they were accomplished or not. Yet we are as anxious about them now as if they were affairs of great importance.

221.

Verily, we do not like crosses if they are not of gold enamelled, and adorned with precious stones.

222.

I am sad and will not speak; this is what parrots do. I am sad, but I speak because charity requires it; thus do spiritual persons. I am despised and I get angry; peacocks and monkeys act thus. I am despised and I rejoice; thus did the Apostles.

223.

Examine whether your heart pleases God?—you must not do it;—but whether his pleases you? yes, truly, for if you look at his Heart, it cannot but please you, it is so sweet, so condescending, so loving towards frail creatures when they recognise their misery, so merciful to the miserable, so kind to the penitent....

224.

Be just; neither excuse nor accuse your poor soul without due reflection, lest by excusing it without reason you render it insolent, or by lightly accusing it you weaken its courage and make it pusillanimous.

225.

How many courtiers there are who go into the presence of the king a hundred times, not to speak to him or listen to him, but merely to be seen by him, and to show by this assiduity that they are his servants. When, then, you come into the presence of our Lord, speak to Him if you can; if you cannot, remain and show yourself to Him, and do not be anxious to do any more.

226.

You do nothing in meditation, you tell me. But what should you do if not just what you are doing, that is, presenting and representing your misery and nothingness to God? The most efficacious appeal a beggar can make is to expose to our eyes his ulcers and necessities.

227.

But sometimes you do not even do this, and you remain before Him like a phantom or statue. Well, that is something. In the palaces of princes and kings there are statues which are only meant to gratify the eyes of the king; content yourself with a similar service in the presence of God. He will animate the statue when it pleases Him. Were we to ask the statue if it desired anything it would answer, "No; I am where my master placed me, and his pleasure is the sole happiness of my being."

228.

Ah! but it is a good prayer, and a good method of keeping one's self in the presence of God, to wait upon his will and good pleasure.

229.

As for me, I think that we keep ourselves in the presence of God even while we sleep, for we go to sleep in his presence and by his will. And when we wake we find that He is beside us, that He has not stirred from us, nor we from Him; therefore we have kept ourselves in his presence, though with closed eyes.

230.

When a certain cross is given to you alone it is of more value, and it should be dearer to you because of its rarity.

231.

God be praised! God or nothing; for all that is not God is nothing, or worse than nothing.

232.

Do not turn your eyes on your infirmities and incapacity, except to humble yourself; never let them discourage you.

233.

Finally, do not be angry, or at least troubled because you have been troubled; do not be overcome because you have allowed yourself to be overcome; do not be disquieted because you have allowed yourself to be disquieted by angry passions; but take your heart and place it gently in the hands of our Lord and ask Him to cure it; meanwhile, do all you can to renew and strengthen your good resolutions.

234.

The highest degree of humility is not only to recognise but to love our abjection. I am guilty of a blunder; it brings humiliation upon me; good. I am guilty of immoderate anger; I am sorry for the offence against God, and very glad that it proves me vile, abject, and miserable.

235.

If envy could reign in the kingdom of eternal love, the angels would envy the sufferings of God for man, and the sufferings of man for God.

236.

Do not be troubled about not making acts of virtue well; for, as I told you, they do not cease to be very good, even when made languidly and wearily as if by force. You can only give God what you have, and in this season of affliction you have no other action to offer Him.

237.

You will be very happy if you receive with a filial and loving heart what our Lord sends you from a heart so paternal in its care of your perfection.

238.

I will not tell you not to regard your afflictions, for your impulsive heart will answer, "I cannot but consider them, they make themselves so keenly felt;" but I tell you to look at them through the cross, and you will find them so small, or at least so agreeable, that you will rather endure their suffering than all consolations without them.

239.

Right sadness speaks thus: "I am miserable, vile, and abject; nevertheless God will exercise his mercy towards me, for virtue will be perfected in infirmity."

240.

When our Lord was upon the cross even his enemies declared Him King; when souls are upon the cross they are declared queens.

241.

Ah! do not examine whether what you do is much or little, whether it is done well or ill, provided it be not sin, and provided you have an upright intention to do it for God. Do everything as perfectly as you can; but, once an action is performed, think no more of it, but rather of what there is to be done.

242.

We should equally resolve upon two things: first, to bring the utmost fidelity to the fulfilment of our exercises; second, to be in no way troubled, disquieted, or astonished if we sometimes fail; for the first comes from our fidelity, which should always be earnest and constantly increasing, and the latter comes from our infirmity.

243.

We must, then, correct our poor heart gently and quietly, and not add to its trouble by the severity of our reprimands. "My heart, my friend," we should say, "in the name of God, take courage; let us keep on and be more watchful in future; let us turn to our Helper and our God." Alas! we must be charitable to our poor soul, and refrain from severity as long as we see that its offences are not deliberate.

244.

Loadstone attracts iron, amber attracts hay and straw; were we hard as iron, or light as straws, we must unite ourselves to this Sovereign Infant Jesus, who truly draws all hearts to Him.

245.

The best thoughts, affections, and aspirations of a great soul are fixed upon the infinitude of eternity; destined as such a soul is for immortality, it finds all that is not eternal too short, all that is not infinite too small.

246.

Yes, speak little, and gently, little and well, little and frankly, little and amiably.

247.

O my God, how beautiful must heaven be, now that the Saviour is its Sun, and his bosom is a fountain of love where the blessed drink at will!

248.

Each one looks therein and sees his name written in characters of love—characters which love alone can read, which love alone has graven.

249.

St. John the Baptist, through obedience, kept himself absent from our Saviour, knowing well that to seek our Saviour outside of obedience was to lose Him.

250.

I leave you to imagine the good odour which this beautiful lily (the Blessed Virgin) spreads in the house of Zachary. What could she give forth but that with which she was filled? And she was filled with Jesus.

251.

My God, I marvel to find that I am so full of myself after so many communions.

252.

There are two kinds of wills: one says, "I would like very much to do good; but it costs a disagreeable effort; it is too difficult;" the other says: "I desire indeed to do good; the will is not wanting, but the power alone stops me." The first fills hell, the second paradise, and it was the latter will which caused Daniel to be called a "man of desires."

253.

I pray you, hide your trouble from yourself as much as you can, and if you feel it, at least do not think about it. You are a little given to dwelling upon it.

254.

You tell me that it is hard to will to do, and to be unable to do. I do not say to you that we must will what we can do, but that before God it is a great deal to be able to will.

255.

What would you do, if you were never to be delivered from your trials? You would say to God: "I am thine; if my miseries are pleasing to Thee multiply them, prolong them." Make friends with your trials, as if you were always to live together, and you will find that when you no longer think of them and cease to be anxious, God will deliver you from them.

256.

No, my dear daughter, I am not troubled as long as our resolutions remain steadfast. Though we were to die, though everything were to be overturned, what would it matter provided they continued firm?

257.

Our night is as brilliant as our day, when God is in our hearts, and our day is night when God is absent from us.

258.

A spirit of indifference helps us in all things, even to making us content during seven weeks, when a father, and a father who loves as I do, and a daughter, such as you, receive no news of each other.

259.

Let the darkness be what it may, we are near the light. Let our impotence be what it may, we are at the feet of the All-powerful.

260.

I shall say nothing of the extent of my affection for you, except that it is incomparable, that it is whiter than the snow, and purer than the sun.

261.

There is nothing which prevents our attaining the perfection of our vocation like desiring another.

262.

I beseech you, my dear daughter, do not fear God as you do, for He does not wish to harm you; love Him fervently, for He wishes to do you a great deal of good.

263.

Our Lord will cause us to enjoy peace when we shall be sufficiently humble to sweetly endure war.

264.

Nothing can equal in merit the offering of our sorrows to Him who saved us by his own.

265.

Dwell very little upon the mixture of self-love in your actions; we should pay no attention to these sallies of self. When we disavow them two or three times a day we have done all that is required. Nor must we violently resist them; a gentle denial is sufficient.

266.

The whole world is not worth a soul, and a soul is worth nothing without its resolutions. We need not be troubled because we are weak, if by trusting in the power and mercy of God we never lose courage; on the contrary, my daughter, I would rather be weak than strong before God, for He takes the weak in his arms, and the strong He leads by the hand.

267.

Believe me, we advance through stormy weather, and under a dark and cloudy sky. It is a better time for travellers than if the sun poured its ardent heat upon us. Courage! light and joy are not within our power, nor any consolation except that which depends upon the will; but while that will is protected by our holy resolutions, and as long as the great seal of the heavenly chancery remains upon our hearts, we have nothing to fear.

268.

Those who spiritually digest Jesus Christ feel that Jesus Christ who is their food is diffused through every part of soul and body. They have Jesus in their mind, in their heart, in their breast, in their eyes, in their hands, in their tongue, in their ears, in their feet. But what does this Saviour do in all these parts? He redresses, purifies, prunes, and vivifies all; the heart loves through Him, the mind understands through Him, the breast breathes through Him, the eyes see through Him, the tongue speaks through Him. Then we can say, "We live now, not we, but Christ Jesus liveth in us." I show you to what we must aspire though we must be content to attain it by degrees.

269.

Let us keep ourselves humble and go to Holy Communion boldly; we shall gradually become accustomed to this heavenly food and learn to digest it to our profit.

270.

Charity, so far from searching for evil, fears to meet it; if she encounter it, she turns away and appears not to see it. She will shut her eyes rather than meet it.

271.

Oh! happy is the mind which sees but two objects, God and self, one of which enraptures it with a sovereign delight, and the other abases it to the extremest abjection.

272.

If what we are doing be necessary, even though it distract our attention from God, we need not be troubled. We are taught to do all our actions for God, and by so doing we keep ourselves in his presence. Beware of thinking it necessary to offer each action to our Lord, for that would interfere with the simplicity of the practice of the Presence of God.

273.

Oh! I pray you, do not fall into the fault of considering the imperfections of others, for it will retard your perfection very much and will injure your soul.

274.

My dear daughter, we must flay the victim if we would have it acceptable to God. In the Old Law, God would accept no victim as a holocaust if it had not first been flayed; in like manner our hearts can never be immolated and sacrificed to God until they shall have been flayed, stripped of their old skin, that is, of their habits, inclinations, repugnances, and superfluous affections.

275.

An act of mortification performed with great repugnance is infinitely suited to strongly advance you in perfection.

276.

My daughters, do not deprive yourselves of Holy Communion because of bitterness of heart; but when you feel it you must draw near to God, to strengthen your heart and unite it to his spirit of meekness.

277.

To pray is to raise the mind to God and converse with Him concerning our interests with a reverent familiarity, and a confidence greater than has the most petted child in its mother, and to talk with Him of all things both high and low, of the things of heaven and the things of earth; it is to open one's heart to Him and pour it out unreservedly to Him; it is to tell Him of our labours, our sins, our desires, and all that is in our soul, and to find our rest with Him as we would with a friend. It is what the Holy Scripture calls "pouring forth one's heart as water before Him."

278.

All should serve charity and charity should serve no one, not even her Beloved, of whom she is not the servant, but the spouse, and to whom she owes love, not service.

279.

Be patient with your trials; our Lord, alas! permits them that you may one day know what you are when left to yourself. Do you not see that the trouble of the day is lighter after the rest of the night? an evident sign that our soul needs but to firmly resign itself to its God, and to become indifferent to serving Him amid thorns or roses.

280.

Be a little lamb, a little dove, quite simple, sweet, and amiable, unquestioning and frank. Love this good God who loves you so much.

281.

Be not too tender towards yourself; avoid weeping and complaints; endeavour to be free and detached from yourself, in order to be wholly under the guidance of God's hand, for where his spirit is there is also liberty.

282.

I see your childish tears and troubles. Know, then, that all our childishness comes from this: that we forget the maxims of the saints, who warn us that we must act as if we were daily to begin anew the labour of our advancement; we shall not be so much astonished to find miseries and faults to correct in ourselves. The work we have undertaken is never finished; we must continually begin over again with a good heart.

283.

There is and can be nothing which I cannot do, inasmuch as I place all my confidence in God, who can do all things, and with this confidence the soul courageously undertakes all that it is commanded, however difficult it may be.

284.

Live joyously, my dearest daughters, in the midst of your holy occupations. When the atmosphere is heavy in the midst of aridity, labour independently of your heart by the practice of a holy abjection and humility.

285.

We shall never possess perfect sweetness and complete charity, if they be not exercised in spite of repugnance, aversion, and disgust. True peace does not consist in not combating but in conquering.

286.

It should be a source of humiliation to us that we are so little master of ourselves, and so fond of our ease. Our Saviour did not come to seek his ease or comfort, either spiritual or temporal, but to deny, to combat Himself, and to die.

287.

Do not allow yourself to yield in any way to sadness, which is the enemy to devotion. What, then, should sadden a soul which serves Him who shall be our joy forever?

288.

Our Lord revealed to Blessed Angela that there is no good so pleasing to Him as that which is done by force; that is, the good which a resolute will effects and offers Him by working against the weight of the flesh, and the repugnances in the inferior part of the soul, and in spite of sadness, aridity, and interior desolation.

289.

What can I say to you on the return of your miseries, save that as the enemy returns we must resume our arms and bring back our courage, in order to fight more valiantly than ever?

290.

Beware of yielding to any kind of distrust, for the heavenly goodness does not permit you to fall in order to abandon you, but to humble you, and teach you to keep a firmer and closer hold of the hand of his mercy.

291.

What happiness to serve God in the desert without manna, without water, with no consolation save that of being under his guidance, and suffering for Him!

292.

When you meet with some contradiction, take your resolutions and place them in the wounds of our Lord, and pray Him to preserve them and you with them; then wait in these blessed retreats until the tempest has past.

293.

The throes and pangs of spiritual birth are painful to nature; our souls must give birth not exteriorly, but interiorly to the sweetest, the most pleasing, the most beautiful child that could be desired. It is the good Jesus whom we must form within ourselves. Courage! we must suffer much that He may be born in us.

294.

You always examine too much to discover whence your sadness comes. We must not be so curious as to wish to know the cause of the diversity of states in this life. And in what way shall we show our love for Him who suffered so much for us, if not by patiently enduring aversions, repugnances, and struggles?

295.

We must cast our heart among the thorns of difficulties, allow it to be transpierced with the lance of contradictions, steeped with gall and vinegar; in a word, feed on absinthe and bitterness, since God wills it.

296.

I desire that you should continue the exercise of getting rid of self by abandoning yourself to our Lord, to the guide of your soul. Say: "I earnestly wish it, Lord; tear, wrest from me without hesitation all that burdens my heart. I except nothing; wrest me from myself! O self! I abandon thee for ever."

297.

You must abide like a poor miserable creature before the throne of Divine Mercy, and remain there wholly stripped of all action and of all affection to creatures, and make yourself indifferent to all things.

298.

How beautiful it is to renounce esteem of self, to renounce what we are, our own will, all complacency in the creature, and, in short, all of self. We must bury this human self in an eternal abandonment, that we may never more see or know it as we have seen and known it.

299.

The virtues which grow in prosperity are of little value; those which are born in the midst of afflictions are strong and firm. In this life God usually allows his children and faithful servants only the honour of suffering much and carrying their cross after Him.

300.

A heart indifferent to all things is like a ball of wax in the hands of God, capable of receiving all the impressions of his eternal good pleasure. It does not place its love in the things which God wills but in the will of God which decrees them.

301.

To belong wholly to God say adieu to all that is not God.

302.

A monastery is an academy of strict correction, where each one should allow himself to be treated, planed, and polished so that all the angles being effaced he may be joined, united, and fastened to the will of God.

303.

It is an evident sign of perfection to wish to be corrected, for the principal fruit of humility is to show us the need we have of correction.

304.

Does God look upon you with love? What a subject to be in doubt about! In his goodness He looks down with love upon the most terrible sinner, have he never so little true desire to be converted.

305.

When shall we become wholly dead to ourselves in the sight of God, and live that new life in which we shall no longer wish to do anything of ourselves, but leave God to do all that He will through us, and let his living will act upon ours, wholly dead in his love?

306.

Jesus our Heart, our Heart of Hearts, lovingly watches over us.

307.

Rest your spirit upon the stone which was represented by the one beneath the head of Jacob, for it is the same upon which St. John reposed on the day when his Master manifested the excess of his love.

308.

Behold St. Peter; fear is a greater evil than the evil which is feared; it would have caused him to perish in the waters had not his Master saved him. Oh! child of little faith, fear not! You are walking on the waters, in the midst of the wind and waves, but it is with Jesus; if fear seizes you cry loudly, "Lord, save me or I perish!" He will extend his hand to you; clasp it firmly and go on joyously.

309.

Yes, abandonment to God in interior and exterior suffering is excellent. Oh! how good it is to live but in God, to work but in God, to rejoice but in God.

310.

When we are in doubt of not having done our duty, or of having offended God, we must humble ourselves, beg God to forgive us, and start afresh. Pure love of God says to us: "Unfaithful one, humble thyself, rely upon the mercy of God, ask pardon, and after renewed promises of fidelity and love, continue on in the pursuit of thy perfection."

311.

I must tell you that you are now dead to the world. This is a part of the holocaust; there remain two other parts, one of which is to remove the skin of the victim, divesting your heart of self, cutting off or getting rid of all the impressions of nature and of creatures; and the other, to burn and reduce your self-love to ashes, and to convert your whole soul into flames of heavenly love.

312.

You should be particularly careful to lean wholly to the side of humility, since you are so much inclined to pride and self-esteem.

313.

Let us humble ourselves and speak of our wounds and miseries at the door of the temple of divine piety; but remember to show them with joy, and be perfectly happy to appear in want and despoiled of all things, in order that our Lord may fill you with his grace.

314.

Be sweet and affable to all except to those who would take from thee thy glory, which is thy misery and thy absolute poverty: "I glory in my infirmities," says the Apostle; "it is good for me to die, rather than that any man should make my glory void." See, he would rather die than lose his infirmities.

315.

Yes, you must keep your misery and lowliness, for God looks down upon it. Men look at the exterior, God looks at the heart; if He sees the lowliness of your heart He will give us great graces. This humility preserves chastity; that is why the soul of the spouse is called the Lily of the Valley.

316.

Keep yourself joyously humble before God, but maintain an equally joyous humility before the world. Be very glad that men make no account of you. If you have their esteem laugh at it joyously; if they esteem you not, console yourself that, as regards you at least, the world judges truly.

317.

I am truly like those fathers who never tire speaking with their children of means for their advancement. But what shall I say to you to this end? Be always very lowly; humble yourself more and more every day. This is true greatness.

318.

I have gotten the habit of recommending all who address themselves to me to lift up their hearts, as the Church tells us in the Holy Sacrifice of the Mass. A heart thus generously lifted up is always humble, for it is established in truth and not in vanity; it is sweet and peaceful, for it makes no account of what could trouble it.

319.

When I say that the heart is sweet and peaceful, I do not mean that it does not suffer and feel affliction. No, certainly, I do not say that; but I say that it meets sufferings, trials, and tribulations with such a strong will to bear them for God, that all its bitterness is full of peace and tranquillity.

320.

It is a great part of our perfection to bear with one another in our imperfections. How can we, in fact, practise love for our neighbour, if not by this forbearance?

321.

Our heart must be kind and gentle towards our neighbour, and full of affection for him, particularly when he is wearisome and displeasing to us, for then we find nothing in him to make us love him but respect for our Saviour.

322.

If your heart be in heaven the winds of the earth cannot move it. No action of the world can harm him who has renounced the world.

323.

Speak of yourself as little as possible; this I tell you earnestly; remember it and pay attention to it. If you are imperfect, humble yourself and do not speak of it.

324.

We must die between the two pillows of humility and confidence.

325.

We must fortify our courage, and never give up because of obstacles, but fight valiantly, astonished neither at the number of our enemies nor the duration of the struggle.

326.

Lord, command my soul all that Thou wilt, and give me strength to obey. Thou hast begun in me the work of my perfection, and I can never doubt that thy goodness will achieve it, if I faithfully co-operate with Thee.

327.

In what do you think the greatness of courage consists? It is in the humility of courage, and yours will be greater in proportion to the humility in which you possess it, that is, in proportion to your little esteem of yourself.

328.

Recall to mind the words so admirably impressed upon the hearts of the apostles by our Saviour: "Unless you be converted and become as little children, you shall not enter into the kingdom of heaven." Verily, if we would attain perfection we must be like little children in our courage, that is, humble, gentle, docile, and easily turned to any purposes.

329.

If you speak, speak of God; if you are silent, speak to God.

330.

I would rather be a gnat by the will of God than a seraph by my own.

331.

Our gentleness with our neighbour must be carried to extreme, even to foolishness, and we must never retaliate; believe me, if we lose something by this, our Lord will make it up elsewhere.

332.

Courage, my very dear daughter: behold, you are at last upon the sacred altar to be sacrificed, immolated, consumed before the face of the living God. Truly, this day must be counted as one of the days which the Lord has made.

333.

Ah! how happy are these beloved hearts of my daughters, in having left for a few years the false liberty of the world to enjoy eternally the enviable slavery which takes away no liberty, save that which would prevent us from being truly free.

334.

I know the state of your soul very well, and I seem to see it always before me with its little emotions of sadness, surprise, and disquiet—emotions which continue to trouble it, because it has not yet cast deep enough the foundations of love of the cross and abjection.

335.

No, my dear daughter, it is not necessary to the practice of virtues to be continually mindful of all of them; that would only embarrass your thoughts and your affections. Humility and charity are the mother cords to which all the others are attached: one is the highest, the other the lowest. The safety of a whole edifice depends upon the foundation and the roof. These are the mother virtues, which the others follow as little chickens do the mother hen.

336.

I have just spoken of you with our Lord, but I dare not absolutely ask for your deliverance; for if it please Him to flay the victim, it is not for me to desire that He should not; but I implore Him to hold you by the hand as He has always done.

337.

God be praised! Live, Jesus! We must bear our cross; whoever bears it best, is through it made the stronger.

338.

There never was a saint who did not experience both ecstasy and rapture in life and its operations by overcoming himself and his natural inclinations.

339.

Whoever has a spirit of prayer despatches more business in an hour than others in several, and wholly at leisure hastens to his rest, which is to treat with God; but God only communicates Himself to the obedient.

340.

Never lose your interior peace for anything, whatever it may be, even though everything be overturned about you; for what are all the things of this life compared to peace of heart?

341.

Under all circumstances, be invariable in the resolution to adhere with great simplicity and unity to God, by a perfectly trustful love, abandoning yourself to the mercy of love and the paternal care which His Providence has of you.

342.

Remain unalterable in a holy nudity of spirit, never assuming any care, desire, affection, or pretension whatever. Our Lord loves you, He wishes you to be wholly his; let no arms but his support you, rest upon no other breast but his.

343.

We must descend to earth to regulate the necessities of this life, but in all things our heart should relish only the dew of God's pleasure, and refer all to the praise of God.

344.

If we love our sweet Saviour let us feed his lambs, since it is a mark of faithful love;—but with what must we feed these dear sheep? With love itself, for they will either not live at all, or they will live upon love.

345.

He who would lay up virtues without humility is like one who carries a precious dust in his hand exposed to the wind. The great secret of maintaining true devotion is to have great humility. Be humble and God will be with you. God is pleased to dwell in a heart deepened by humility, docile through simplicity, and great through charity. He who is truly humble desires to be humbled. Humility produces generosity. Remember, my dear daughter, that the keenest humiliations are those which are least visible.

346.

We must change from one place to another without changing our love or the object of our love. Be indifferent to all occupation in the midst of different occupations. Be uninfluenced by affairs, and remain equally for God in all things.

347.

How happy we shall be if one day we change self into that holy love which shall make us one, and entirely free us from all complexity of affairs, so that we shall have at heart only the sovereign unity of his Holy Trinity.

348.

Curiosity, ambition, restlessness, and forgetfulness of the end for which we are in this world are the cause of our having more impediments than works, more bustle than business, more undertakings than results. And these incumbrances, these superfluous occupations with which we burden ourselves, are what divert us from God, and not the legitimate exercise of our employments.

349.

Our perfection must be true and solid. For example, though anger is raging within me, though my blood boils, I will not cease to be as gracious and gentle as it is possible to be, and all the reasons which nature urges for its release I will strangle as she presents them, I will not listen to one of them. This is true virtue, true gentleness. Ah! God gives you occasion to practise patience. Would you let it escape you? Perhaps you may never in life meet with such another opportunity.

350.

Courage, my poor mind! Let us reject all discourse, research, inquiry; let us become more simple, and be rid of this tiresome care of self; let us confine ourselves to the simple view of God and our own nothingness. Let us steadily lean upon the results of the sovereign will, even when we fall, for the dear Jesus will give us the necessary sentiments. O mind, one is never wholly master of thee.... Thou wouldst know all in spite of us. O my God, stop this miserable wanderer!

351.

The saints did not abound so much in sensible sentiments, they worked according to the lights and truths of faith. Ah! let us be ever wholly detached from everything before God, taking no trouble for what comes to us. Let all that is not God be as nothing to us. Let us contemplate the infinite goodness of God and forget ourselves. Let us immolate all our affections to Jesus Christ.

352.

Condescending to the humour of others, bearing with rudeness and tiresome manners on the part of our neighbour, victories over our own humours and passions, renouncing our smallest inclinations, efforts against our aversions and repugnances, a continual endeavour to maintain the peace of our soul, a kind and amiable manner of receiving censures upon our condition, our life, our conversation, are all more fruitful to our soul than we can imagine, provided love for God be the motive which animates us.

353.

Whenever I enter a place consecrated to our august Queen, I experience a thrill of love which tells me that I am with my mother, for I feel that I am the child of her who is called the refuge of sinners.

354.

Away from me those who love severity, for I will have none of it! It is better to be obliged to account to God for too much gentleness than too much severity. Is not God all love? God the Father is the father of the wretched; God the Son is called a lamb; God the Holy Ghost manifests Himself under the form of a dove. If there were anything better than benignity Jesus Christ would have told us, and yet He gives us but two lessons to learn of Him—meekness and humility.

355.

The passport of the daughters of Jesus Christ is peace. The joy of the daughters of Our Lady is peace. We must always be at peace. Know that the virtue of patience is that which most assures us perfection; and if we are to be patient with others, we must be equally so with ourselves. May Jesus be in the midst of thy heart, and thy heart in the midst of Jesus! May Jesus live in thy heart, and thy heart in Jesus! Amen.

356.

Great saints never are guilty of mortal sin, but only of useless, ill-timed, imprudent, and rude actions; slight acts of impatience, slight excesses of joy, of mirth, slight failings in vanity, and other like faults are useless movements and irregularities into which the just fall seven times—that is, very often.

357.

If I want only pure water, what does it matter whether it be brought me in a vase of gold or glass? What is it to me whether the will of God be presented to me in tribulation or consolation, since I desire and seek only the divine will?

358.

A heart indifferent to all things is like a ball of wax in the hands of God, to receive all the impressions of his eternal good pleasure, a heart with no choice, disposed for all things, placing its affection, not in the things which God wills, but in the will of God which decrees them.

359.

Paradise is no more pleasing than the miseries of this world, if the divine good pleasure be equally in the miseries as in paradise. Labour is paradise, if the divine will be found in it, and paradise labour, if the divine will be not in it.

360.

The divine good pleasure is the sovereign object of the detached soul; wherever it sees it, it runs in the odour of its perfumes, unceasingly seeks the places where it most abounds, regardless of all other things.

361.

In the monastery of the devout life each one considers himself a novice, and a lifetime is devoted to a probation according to the rule of the order; it is not the solemnity of the vows but their fulfilment which makes novices professed.

362.

He who ardently loves God does not turn back his gaze upon himself to discover what he is doing, but keeps his heart occupied with God, the object of his love. A heavenly chorister takes so much delight in pleasing God, that he desires no pleasure from the melody of his voice, save as it is pleasing to his Sovereign.

363.

There is nothing so sad as to serve a master who knows nothing of our devotion, or who, if he knows it, gives no sign of being satisfied with it; and it must be a strong love which sustains itself alone, unsupported by any pleasure or aspiration. Thus does it happen in the exercises of sacred love; like deaf choristers we do not hear our own voice, on the contrary, we are oppressed by a thousand fears, and by the uproar which the devil makes about our heart, suggesting that we are not pleasing to our Master, that our love is useless, yea, even false and vain. Oh, my dear Theotime! it is then we must manifest an invincible fidelity to our Saviour, serving Him purely for love of his will, not only without pleasure, but in the midst of this deluge of sadness, terrors, alarms, and temptations.

364.

No, Lord, I wish for no event; for I leave Thee to will it for me as Thou pleasest; but instead of wishing for events I bless Thee for those Thou has ordained. Father, I am thine. I know not what I should wish; it is for Thee to will and do for me all that shall seem to Thee good. "My Father truly loves me, and I am wholly his."

365.

O Jesus! be my sweetness and my honey; sweeten my heart by the sweetness of thine.

366.

To whom is He not good, this Sovereign Love of hearts? Those who taste of his sweetness can never be sated therewith, and those who approach His heart cannot contain their own with praising and blessing Him for ever. Continue to unite yourself more and more to this dear Saviour. Bury your heart in the charity of his, and let us say with all our heart: "May I die and Jesus live; this shall be a happy death if it take place in this life." May you be blessed with the benediction which the Divine Goodness has prepared for hearts which abandon themselves a prey to his sacred and holy love.

367.

You must bow your head and bear yourself contrary to your habits or inclinations. Live humbly before God, amiably with your neighbour, and sweetly with yourself.

368.

Cast your thoughts earnestly upon the shoulders of the Saviour, and He will support and strengthen you. When He calls you to a kind of service which is contrary to your taste, your courage should not be less, but rather more than if your taste concurred with his pleasure, for where there is least of self the work goes best. Do not permit your mind to consider itself, its powers, its inclinations. You must keep your eyes fixed upon the good pleasure of God, and upon Providence.

369.

We must not amuse ourselves with discoursing when we should run, nor with chatting about difficulties when we should conquer them. Say courageously: "I will do much; not I, but the grace of God which is within me."

370.

Hold the cross of our Lord upon your breast, and as long as you firmly clasp it in your arms, the enemy will be at your feet.

371.

Ah! how I would like to see you always transfigured in our Lord! Oh! how beautiful is his face, how sweet his eyes in their wonderful gentleness, and how good it is to be with Him on the mount of glory! It is there we should lodge our affections, and not on this earth, where there is nothing but empty beauty and false vanity.

372.

May God give you strength to break the ties which prevent you from following the heavenly attractions of your heart! Ah! it is sad to see a little bee in the treacherous coils of a spider, but if a favourable wind of grace break these wretched fetters, these unfortunate meshes, why does not this dear bee hasten to disentangle itself and proceed to the making of its sweet honey.

373.

The sting of honey-bees is much more dangerous than that of other bees, and so the machinations of friends against us are exceedingly hard to bear; but we must endure them, bear with them, and finally love them as dear contradictions. We must absolutely, invariably, and inviolably desire only God. But the means of serving Him should be the object of a very feeble desire on our part, so that if one means be taken from us we shall not be greatly affected thereby. Our desire for everything which is not God should be very weak and indifferent.

374.

When we are ill in body we must exact of our minds only acts of submission and acceptance of labour, and acts uniting our will with the good pleasure of God, which acts are formed in the superior part of the soul. As to exterior actions, we must perform them as best we can, even though it be languidly, heavily, and against our inclinations; and to make them acceptable to Divine Love, we must acknowledge, accept, and cherish the holy abjection of our state. In this way you will change the lead of your languor into gold, and that, too, finer gold than your heart could offer in its brightest and happiest moments.

375.

It seems to me that I see your heart before me like a dial placed in the sun, which never moves, while its needle and balance are continually in motion, ever turning towards the beautiful planet; for your heart in like manner remains motionless, while your will is continually turning by means of its good desires towards God.

376.

How is your poor heart? Is it always valiant and vigilant against attacks of sadness? In God's name, do not torment it, even though it wander a little; reprove it gently, and bring it back to the path. You will see that this heart will become a true heart, according to the Heart of God.

377.

Think of that great dereliction which our Master endured, and see how this dear Son, having asked consolation of his good Father, and seeing that He willed not to grant it, thought of it no more, ceased to seek it, but, as if He had never desired it, valiantly and courageously set about the work of our redemption. After you shall have prayed to your Heavenly Father for consolation, if it does not please Him to give it you, cease to think of it, but renew your courage to work out your salvation on the cross, as if you were never to descend therefrom.

378.

O my God! how beautiful, how lovely is this cross! We make every effort to obtain the wood, and we exalt it on the Mount of Calvary. Alas! happy are those who love it and bear it. It will be exalted in heaven, when our Lord shall come to judge the living and the dead, to teach us that heaven is the mansion of crucified souls.

379.

I love independent, vigorous, and sensible souls; for this great sensibility confuses and disquiets the heart, and distracts it from the prayer of loving attention to God, prevents complete resignation, and impedes the perfect destruction of self-love. I am the most affectionate person in the world; and it seems to me that I love nothing but God, and all souls for God.

380.

When a soul aspires to be the spouse of Jesus Christ, it must cast off the old man and clothe itself in the new, by giving up sin, and then cutting off from its life all the superfluities which could divert it from divine love.

381.

As the exercise of purity of heart ends only with life, let us not be troubled at sight of our imperfections. Our perfection consists in combating them, and we cannot combat or vanquish them without feeling and knowing them.

382.

Our Lord is the mysterious tree of desire of which the holy spouse of the canticle speaks. It is to his feet, then, that we must go to breathe a sweeter air, howsoever little the heart may be oppressed by the atmosphere of the world.

383.

We desire to build a great edifice, that is, to erect God's dwelling within us; therefore let us consider whether we have sufficient courage to ruin ourselves, or to let God raze us to the ground that He may rebuild us into a living temple of his Majesty.

384.

Our sole pretentions should be to be united to God, as our Lord was united to his Father when He died on the cross.

385.

Desire nothing, ask nothing, refuse nothing; this practice contains all perfection.

386.

There is a certain simplicity of heart which contains the perfection of all perfections; and it is this simplicity which makes our soul consider God alone, and keep its forces wholly collected within itself, in order to devote itself with all possible fidelity to the observance of his laws, with no wish or desire for anything else.

387.

Recall yourself sometimes to the interior solitude of your heart, and there, removed from all creatures, treat of the affairs of your salvation and your perfection with God, as a friend would speak heart to heart with another.

388.

We retire into God because we aspire to Him, and we aspire to Him that we may retire into Him. Thus the retirement of the heart and the aspiration towards God are one the effect of the other.

389.

Our will can never die, but it sometimes passes beyond the limits of its ordinary life to live wholly in the divine will. This is accomplished when it will not and cannot any longer will anything, but abandons itself without reserve to the good pleasure of Providence: it no longer lives, but the will of God lives in it.

390.

Let us be earnestly attentive to blessing God for all that He shall do, saying: "The Lord gave and the Lord hath taken away; blessed be the name of the Lord." No, Lord, I desire nothing; for I leave Thee to will for me wholly as Thou pleasest; instead of wishing for anything, I bless Thee for what Thou shalt decree.

391.

Hast thou fallen into the net of adversity? Look not at thy misfortunes, or the snares into which thou art taken, but turn to God and leave all to Him. He will care for thee.

392.

We should peacefully abide in our misery and abjection, in the midst of our imperfections and weakness until it shall please God to raise us to the practice of great virtues.

393.

We must live in this world as if our mind were in heaven and our body in the tomb.

394.

Choose the best virtues and not those which are most esteemed; the most excellent, and not the most apparent; the most solid, and not the most fanciful.

395.

If anger or pride attack me, I must do all in my power to incline my heart to humility and meekness, devoting to that end my spiritual exercises, the sacraments and the other virtues.

396.

Do not limit your patience to certain trials, but extend it universally to all that God shall send you, or permit to reach you through any source.

397.

A truly patient man bears, with the same evenness of temper, ignominious trials and those which are honourable. As the sting of bees is more painful than that of flies, so the contradictions we experience at the hands of good people are more trying than those which come from the wicked.

398.

Complain as little as possible of injuries, for it rarely happens that one complains without sin, since our self-love exaggerates in our eyes and hearts the wrongs we have received.

399.

You wish absolutely to form Jesus Christ in you, in your heart, in your works, by a sincere love of his doctrine and a perfect imitation of his life; rest assured it will cost you many pangs; but they will pass away, and the presence of Jesus, who shall live in you, will fill your soul with an ineffable joy which can never be taken from you.

400.

Think frequently of Jesus crucified; consider Him covered with wounds, filled with sadness, despoiled of everything, loaded with maledictions. Then you will acknowledge that your sufferings can in no way compare with his, and that never shall you endure anything in the least degree approaching what He suffered for you.

401.

God's great desire is that we should be perfect, to unite ourselves with Him by the perfect imitation of his sanctity. "Be you therefore perfect, as your Heavenly Father is perfect."

www.ingramcontent.com/pod-product-compliance
Lightning Source LLC
Chambersburg PA
CBHW021146020426
42331CB00005B/924